Growing and Pruning Orchids

Learning Easy ways to Growing Orchids

By

David Birrani

Table of Contents

CHAPTER 1

Orchids

Orchids are a diverse and widespread family of flowering plants, with over 28,000 species and more than 100,000 hybrids and cultivars. They are found in every continent except Antarctica, and thrive in a wide range of habitats including rainforests, deserts, and marshes. Orchids are prized for their beautiful and often elaborate flowers, which come in a stunning variety of colors, shapes, and sizes.

Orchids are members of the Orchidaceae family, which is one of the largest families of flowering plants. They are characterized by their unique reproductive structures, which have evolved to be highly specialized and efficient at pollination. Unlike most other flowering plants, which have male and female reproductive structures in separate flowers, orchids have both male and female reproductive structures in the same flower. This means that orchids are self-fertile, meaning they can fertilize themselves, but they also rely on external pollinators such as bees, moths, and birds to ensure genetic diversity.

Orchids are also known for their intricate and often symbiotic relationships with fungi. Most orchid seeds are tiny and lack the energy reserves needed to germinate and grow into mature plants. Instead, they rely on a symbiotic relationship with a type of fungus to provide them with the nutrients they need to grow. The fungus breaks down complex organic compounds in the soil and provides the orchid seed with simple nutrients that it can absorb. In return, the orchid provides the fungus with sugars and other nutrients that it has synthesized through photosynthesis.

Orchids are cultivated around the world for their aesthetic beauty and commercial value. They are commonly used in the production of perfumes, and their flowers are often used in traditional medicine. Orchids are also popular as ornamental plants and are grown as houseplants or in specialized greenhouses known as orchidariums. Many orchids are rare or endangered in the wild, due to habitat loss and overcollection, and there are numerous conservation efforts aimed at protecting these valuable and ecologically important plants.

In terms of care, orchids can be challenging to grow and require specific conditions to thrive. The most common mistake made by beginners is overwatering. Orchids prefer to be watered infrequently and require good drainage to prevent root rot. They also need a humid environment and should be kept out of direct sunlight. Orchid growers use a variety of techniques to replicate the orchid's natural growing conditions, including misting, using humidifiers, and growing orchids in specialized potting media. With the right care, however, orchids can be long-lived and rewarding plants to grow.

There are many different types of orchids, each with their own unique characteristics and growing requirements. Some popular orchid varieties include Phalaenopsis or "Moth Orchids", Cattleya, Dendrobium, and Vanda. Each type of orchid has its own specific care requirements, such as temperature, humidity, and light levels, so it's important to research and understand the needs of your particular orchid.

In addition to their aesthetic and cultural significance, orchids also have scientific importance. Their unique reproductive structures have long fascinated biologists, and they have been the subject of numerous studies on pollination, symbiosis, and evolution. Orchids have also been used in genetic research, as they have the smallest known plant genome, making them ideal candidates for studying the evolution of complex traits.

In ancient Greece, orchids were associated with virility and were believed to be an aphrodisiac. In China, orchids have been cultivated for over 3,000 years and are associated with elegance, refinement, and fertility. In Japan, orchids are used in traditional tea ceremonies and are considered a symbol of purity and nobility. In many cultures, orchids are also associated with longevity and good fortune.

Orchids have been cultivated for thousands of years, and their cultivation has played an important role in human history. Orchids were prized by ancient civilizations such as the Greeks and Romans, who believed that they possessed healing properties and used them in medicinal remedies. In medieval Europe, orchids were considered a symbol of love and were used in love potions and spells.

During the 19th century, orchids became a popular ornamental plant in Europe and North America, and a lucrative trade developed around their collection and cultivation.

Many orchids were collected from the wild, leading to habitat destruction and endangerment of many orchid species. Today, the commercial orchid industry is a multi-billion-dollar global enterprise, with orchids being grown and traded around the world.

Despite their popularity and commercial value, many orchids are threatened by habitat loss, climate change, and overcollection. In response to these threats, numerous conservation efforts have been undertaken to protect endangered orchid species and their habitats. These efforts include habitat restoration, captive breeding, and public education campaigns aimed at raising awareness of the importance of orchids and the need to protect them.

In addition to their conservation value, orchids have many practical applications. Orchid extracts are used in the production of cosmetics, perfumes, and food flavorings, and their roots are used in traditional medicine. Orchids also have potential as a source of new drugs, as they contain a wide variety of bioactive compounds with potential therapeutic properties.

orchids are a diverse and fascinating group of plants with a long and rich history. They are prized for their beauty, cultural significance, and scientific importance, and their conservation is an important priority for ensuring the continued survival of these valuable and ecologically important plants.

CHAPTER 2

Steps for Growing and Pruning Orchids

1. Choose the right type of orchid for your environment and skill level. Different orchids have different requirements, so it's important to research the needs of the specific orchid you want to grow. For example, some orchids prefer cooler temperatures, while others require more humidity.

2. Provide the right amount of light. Most orchids prefer bright, indirect light. Avoid direct sunlight, as this can

scorch the leaves. However, some orchids, such as cattleyas, require more direct sunlight to flower.

3. Maintain the right temperature range. Orchids generally prefer temperatures between 60-80°F (15-27°C) during the day and 50-70°F (10-21°C) at night. However, some orchids, such as phalaenopsis, prefer slightly warmer temperatures.

4. Water orchids once a week, allowing the potting mix to dry out slightly between waterings. Overwatering can lead to root rot, while underwatering can cause the leaves to wilt and dry out.

Watering frequency may vary depending on the type of orchid and the environment it's growing in.

5. Use a well-draining potting mix that allows air to circulate around the roots. Orchids require good air circulation to thrive. A mix of bark, perlite, and sphagnum moss is commonly used for orchids.

6. Repot orchids every 1-2 years to refresh the potting mix and provide room for growth. Choose a pot that is only slightly larger than the current pot. Repotting is best done in the spring just before new growth emerges.

7. Fertilize orchids regularly with a balanced fertilizer (such as 20-20-20) at half-strength every 2-3 weeks during the growing season (spring and summer). Some orchids, such as cymbidiums, require a different fertilizer ratio.

8. Increase humidity levels to 50-70%, especially in dry environments. You can do this by misting the leaves or placing a tray of water near the orchid. Some orchids, such as dendrobiums, require less humidity.

9. Avoid placing orchids near cold drafts or heating vents. Drastic changes in

temperature can stress the orchid and lead to problems. Orchids prefer stable temperatures.

10.		Use a tray of water or a humidifier to increase humidity levels if necessary. This is especially important if you live in a dry climate. You can also use a humidity tray to increase moisture around the orchid.

11.		Provide proper air circulation by placing orchids in a location with good ventilation. This helps prevent the buildup of moisture and reduces the risk of disease. Avoid placing orchids in a closed environment, such as a terrarium.

12.   Use a fan to circulate air around orchids if necessary. This can be especially helpful in humid climates. A gentle breeze helps to prevent the growth of mold and bacteria.

13.   Avoid overcrowding orchids, as this can lead to poor air circulation and increased risk of disease. Give each orchid enough space to grow. If you have multiple orchids, space them out evenly.

14.   Monitor orchids for signs of pests and disease, such as yellowing leaves,

brown spots, or webbing. Catching problems early can prevent them from spreading and causing more damage. You can use natural remedies or chemical treatments to control pests and diseases.

15.   Keep orchids away from other plants. Some plants can harbor pests or diseases that can spread to your orchids. It's also a good idea to keep your orchids away from areas where pesticides or other chemicals are used

16.   Remove dead or yellowing leaves regularly. This helps to keep the orchid looking healthy and prevents

the buildup of rot or disease. Use a clean, sharp pair of scissors to make a clean cut.

17.   Trim away any damaged or dead roots. Over time, orchid roots can become damaged or die off. Trim away any dead roots using a sterile tool to prevent the spread of disease. Healthy roots should be firm and plump.

18.   Cut back old flower spikes once they have finished blooming. This helps to redirect the orchid's energy into new growth instead of producing seeds. Use a sterile tool to make a clean cut just above a node or dormant bud.

19.	Divide orchids when they outgrow their pot or become crowded. This is typically done when the orchid has at least 3-4 new growths or "eyes". Divide the orchid carefully, making sure each division has at least 3-4 healthy roots and a new growth.

20.	Sterilize your pruning tools regularly to prevent the spread of disease. Use rubbing alcohol or a solution of 10% bleach and water to sterilize your scissors, clippers, or other tools. Wipe down the tools between each use.

21.	Avoid pruning orchids during their dormant period. Orchids typically go through a period of rest after blooming. During this time, avoid pruning or repotting the orchid, as it may be more vulnerable to stress.

22.	Use pruning to shape the orchid or control its growth. You can prune back the tips of the leaves to encourage branching or cut back the length of a stem to promote new growth. However, be careful not to remove too much growth at once.

23.	Prune away any flowers or growths that show

signs of disease. This can help prevent the spread of disease to other parts of the orchid. Make sure to sterilize your tools before and after pruning.

24.	Use pruning to control the size of the orchid. If you want to keep your orchid a certain size, you can prune it back to prevent it from becoming too large or overgrown. Be careful not to remove too much growth at once.

25.	Take your time when pruning orchids. It's important to make clean, precise cuts to prevent damage to the orchid. Use sharp, sterile tools and take your time to make sure you're pruning the right parts of the plant.

26.   Don't be afraid to prune orchids that have finished blooming. Orchids are resilient plants that can handle pruning. Removing old flower spikes and dead growth will help promote new growth and ensure a healthy orchid.

27.   Avoid pruning orchids during times of stress or illness. If your orchid is showing signs of stress or illness, such as yellowing leaves or a lack of growth, it's

best to hold off on pruning until it has recovered.

28.   Consider using a specialized orchid fertilizer to promote healthy growth. Orchids require specific nutrients to thrive, and regular fertilization can help encourage new growth and blooms.

29.   Be cautious when pruning orchids with thick, fleshy roots. These roots are vital to the plant's health and should not be trimmed unless absolutely necessary.

30.   Keep your orchid's growing conditions consistent. Orchids thrive in stable conditions, so make

sure to keep the temperature, humidity, and light levels consistent to promote healthy growth and blooms.

31.   When repotting orchids, prune away any dead or damaged roots before placing the plant in a new pot.

32.   If you're unsure about how to prune your orchid, seek advice from a knowledgeable orchid grower or a horticulturalist.

33.   Be patient when waiting for your orchid to bloom. Some orchids can take several years to bloom, so don't be discouraged if you don't see blooms right away.

34.	Don't overwater your orchids. Overwatering can lead to root rot and other issues. Instead, wait until the top inch of soil is dry before watering again.

35.	Keep an eye out for pests and diseases. Regular monitoring can help you catch and treat any issues early on, preventing them from spreading to other parts of the orchid.

36.	When pruning, make sure to use a clean, sharp tool to prevent damage to the plant.

37.	Avoid pruning orchids during periods of extreme

heat or cold, as this can stress the plant.

38.   If your orchid has outgrown its current pot, consider repotting it before pruning to give it more space to grow.

39.   Be mindful of the type of orchid you're pruning, as different species may require different pruning methods.

40.   Don't be afraid to experiment with different pruning techniques to find what works best for your orchids. With time and practice, you'll become a pro at pruning orchids.

CHAPTER 3

Types of Orchids

1. Phalaenopsis (Moth orchids): These are one of the most popular orchids for indoor growing due to their ease of care and stunning blooms. They are often available in white, pink, yellow, and purple colors, and produce flowers that can last for several weeks. Phalaenopsis orchids prefer bright, indirect light and should be watered deeply but infrequently.

2. Cattleya: These orchids produce large, showy flowers in a range of colors, including

pink, purple, and white. They require more sunlight than some other orchids and should be watered deeply but allowed to dry out slightly between waterings. Cattleya orchids can be more challenging to grow than some other varieties, but their stunning blooms make them well worth the effort.

3. Dendrobium: These orchids are known for their long, thin stems and clusters of small, delicate flowers. They are available in a wide range of colors and are often fragrant. Dendrobium orchids prefer bright, indirect light and should be watered deeply but

allowed to dry out slightly between waterings.

4. Oncidium (Dancing Lady orchids): These orchids produce clusters of small, colorful flowers that resemble dancing ladies. They come in a range of colors, including yellow, orange, and pink, and prefer bright, indirect light. Oncidium orchids should be watered deeply but allowed to dry out slightly between waterings.

5. Paphiopedilum (Lady Slipper orchids): These orchids have unique, slipper-shaped blooms and are known for their hardiness. They are

available in a range of colors
and patterns and prefer
bright, indirect light.
Paphiopedilum orchids
should be watered deeply but
allowed to dry out slightly
between waterings.

6. Miltonia (Pansy orchids):
   These orchids produce large,
   flat blooms that resemble
   pansies and come in a variety
   of colors. They prefer bright,
   indirect light and should be
   watered deeply but allowed
   to dry out slightly between
   waterings.

7. Vanda: These orchids have
   long, thin stems and produce
   large, showy flowers in a
   range of colors. They prefer

bright, indirect light and require high humidity. Vanda orchids should be watered frequently, with their roots being soaked for several minutes at a time.

8. Brassia (Spider orchids): These orchids have long, thin petals that resemble spider legs and come in a variety of colors, including yellow, green, and brown. They prefer bright, indirect light and should be watered deeply but allowed to dry out slightly between waterings.

9. Zygopetalum: These orchids have beautiful, fragrant blooms in shades of purple, green, and white. They prefer

bright, indirect light and should be watered deeply but allowed to dry out slightly between waterings.

10.   Masdevallia: These orchids have unique, tube-shaped blooms in a range of colors, including red, orange, and purple. They prefer cooler temperatures and high humidity, and should be watered frequently to keep their roots moist.

11.   Cambria: These orchids are a hybrid of several different orchid species and produce large, showy blooms in a range of colors. They prefer bright, indirect light and should be watered deeply

but allowed to dry out slightly between waterings.

12.	Epidendrum: These orchids produce clusters of small, colorful flowers in shades of pink, purple, and red. They are easy to grow and prefer bright, indirect light and well-draining soil. Epidendrum orchids should be watered deeply but allowed to dry out slightly between waterings.

13.	Laelia: These orchids have large, showy blooms in shades of pink, purple, and white. They prefer bright, indirect light and should be watered deeply but allowed to dry out slightly between waterings.

14.   Vanda: These orchids have large, colorful blooms in shades of blue, purple, and red. They prefer bright, indirect light and high humidity, and should be watered frequently to keep their roots moist.

15.   Stanhopea: These orchids have unique, fragrant blooms that grow from the base of the plant. They prefer bright, indirect light and high humidity, and should be watered frequently to keep their roots moist.

16.   Ludisia (Jewel orchids): These orchids have beautiful, patterned leaves in shades of green, purple, and silver. They prefer bright, indirect light and

should be watered deeply but allowed to dry out slightly between waterings.

17.   Maxillaria: These orchids have small, delicate flowers in shades of yellow, orange, and brown. They prefer bright, indirect light and should be watered deeply but allowed to dry out slightly between waterings.

18.   Brassavola: These orchids have fragrant, white blooms that grow in clusters. They prefer bright, indirect light and should be watered deeply but allowed to dry out slightly between waterings.

19.   Angraecum: These orchids have unique, long-lasting

flowers in shades of white and green. They prefer bright, indirect light and high humidity, and should be watered frequently to keep their roots moist.

20. Encyclia: These orchids have small, fragrant flowers in shades of pink, purple, and yellow. They prefer bright, indirect light and should be watered deeply but allowed to dry out slightly between waterings.

21. Zygopetalum: These orchids have unique, fragrant flowers in shades of green, purple, and brown. They prefer bright, indirect light and high humidity, and should be watered

frequently to keep their roots moist.

22.   Pleurothallis: These orchids have small, intricate flowers in a range of colors, including yellow, red, and purple. They prefer bright, indirect light and high humidity, and should be watered frequently to keep their roots moist.

23.   Dracula: These orchids have small, unique flowers that resemble miniature Dracula faces. They prefer bright, indirect light and high humidity, and should be watered frequently to keep their roots moist.

24.   Sobralia: These orchids have large, showy flowers in shades

of pink, purple, and white. They prefer bright, indirect light and high humidity, and should be watered frequently to keep their roots moist.

25.　Lycaste: These orchids have large, fragrant flowers in shades of pink, yellow, and white. They prefer bright, indirect light and should be watered deeply but allowed to dry out slightly between waterings.

26.　Epidendrum: These orchids have small, delicate flowers in shades of pink, orange, and yellow. They prefer bright, indirect light and should be watered deeply but allowed to dry out slightly between waterings.

27.   Bulbophyllum: These orchids have unique, intricate flowers in a range of colors, including red, orange, and yellow. They prefer bright, indirect light and high humidity, and should be watered frequently to keep their roots moist.

28.   Gongora: These orchids have long, slender flowers in shades of pink, purple, and green. They prefer bright, indirect light and high humidity, and should be watered frequently to keep their roots moist.

29.   Laeliocattleya: These orchids are a cross between the Laelia and Cattleya orchids, and produce large, showy flowers in shades of pink, purple, and

white. They prefer bright, indirect light and should be watered deeply but allowed to dry out slightly between waterings.

30. Sarcochilus: These orchids have delicate, fragrant flowers in shades of pink, white, and purple. They prefer bright, indirect light and should be watered deeply but allowed to dry out slightly between waterings.

31. Coelogyne: These orchids have large, fragrant flowers in shades of white, pink, and yellow. They prefer bright, indirect light and high humidity, and should be watered

frequently to keep their roots moist.

32. Tolumnia: These orchids have small, delicate flowers in a wide range of colors, including pink, purple, and yellow. They prefer bright, indirect light and should be watered deeply but allowed to dry out slightly between waterings.

33. Calanthe: These orchids have large, showy flowers in shades of pink, purple, and white. They prefer bright, indirect light and should be watered deeply but allowed to dry out slightly between waterings.

CHAPTER 4

Awakening an Orchid

Awakening an orchid refers to bringing it out of its dormancy period and encouraging it to start growing again.

1. Check the roots: The first step in awakening an orchid is to check the roots. Healthy roots should be plump and firm, while unhealthy roots will appear shriveled or mushy. If the roots are healthy, the orchid is ready to be awakened.

2. Increase light: Orchids need bright but indirect light to grow. Place the orchid in a

spot where it will receive plenty of light, but avoid placing it in direct sunlight as this can scorch the leaves.

3. Adjust temperature: Orchids require warm temperatures during the day and cooler temperatures at night to stimulate growth. Aim for a daytime temperature of 65-80°F and a nighttime temperature of 55-65°F.

4. Increase humidity: Orchids thrive in high humidity environments. Use a humidifier or place a tray of water near the orchid to increase humidity levels. Alternatively, you can group

orchids together to create a humid microclimate.

5. Watering: Orchids require regular watering during their growing season. Water the orchid when the potting mix feels dry to the touch, but avoid overwatering as this can cause the roots to rot.

6. Fertilizing: Fertilize the orchid with a balanced orchid fertilizer during the growing season to provide the necessary nutrients for growth.

7. Pruning: If the orchid has dead or damaged leaves or stems, prune them back to encourage new growth.

8. Repotting: If the orchid has outgrown its current pot or the potting mix has broken down, repot it in fresh potting mix to provide the necessary nutrients and space for growth.

9. Check for pests: Before awakening an orchid, it is important to check for any signs of pest infestation. Common orchid pests include mealybugs, scale insects, and spider mites. If you notice any pests, treat the orchid with an appropriate insecticide before attempting to awaken it.

10. Choose the right potting mix: Orchids require

a special potting mix that allows for adequate drainage and aeration. Look for a mix specifically formulated for orchids or make your own using a combination of bark, sphagnum moss, and perlite.

11. Consider a growth hormone: Some orchids may benefit from the application of a growth hormone to encourage new growth. Follow the instructions carefully when using a growth hormone and avoid over-applying.

12. Use a balanced fertilizer: Orchids require a balanced fertilizer that contains equal parts nitrogen,

phosphorus, and potassium. Use a fertilizer specifically formulated for orchids and follow the recommended application rate.

13. Monitor watering: Overwatering is a common problem with orchids. To avoid this, water the orchid only when the potting mix is dry to the touch, and ensure that the pot has adequate drainage holes.

14. Provide proper ventilation: Orchids require good air circulation to prevent the growth of mold and fungal diseases. Avoid placing the orchid in a stagnant area and ensure that

the room has proper ventilation.

15.   Choose the right location: Orchids should be placed in a location with plenty of bright, indirect light. Avoid placing the orchid in a location with direct sunlight, as this can cause the leaves to burn.

16.   Control temperature fluctuations: Orchids prefer a stable temperature and do not respond well to sudden changes. Keep the orchid away from doors or windows that may cause sudden temperature fluctuations.

17.   Humidity trays: If you live in a dry climate, consider

using a humidity tray to increase the humidity around the orchid. Fill a tray with pebbles and water, and place the orchid pot on top.

18.	Monitor for signs of stress: Orchids can become stressed if they are not provided with the proper growing conditions. Watch for signs of stress, such as yellowing or dropping leaves, and adjust the growing conditions as necessary.

19.	Use a fungicide: Orchids are susceptible to fungal diseases, which can be prevented with the use of a fungicide. Apply the fungicide according to the instructions on the label.

20.　　Avoid repotting during dormancy: If the orchid is in dormancy, avoid repotting it as this can cause stress and interrupt the natural growth cycle. Wait until the orchid begins to show signs of new growth before repotting.

CHAPTER 5

How to Water Orchids

Watering orchids correctly is essential for their growth and health.

1. Know your orchid: Different orchid species have different water requirements. Some prefer to dry out between waterings, while others prefer to be kept moist. Research your specific orchid species to determine its watering needs.

2. Water when the potting mix is dry: Orchids should be watered when the potting mix is almost dry. This usually

means watering once a week
or every two weeks,
depending on the orchid
species and growing
conditions. Avoid
overwatering, as this can lead
to root rot.

3. Water in the morning:
Watering in the morning
allows the orchid to dry out
during the day, which
reduces the risk of fungal
growth. Avoid watering in
the evening or at night.

4. Use room temperature water:
Orchids prefer water that is at
room temperature, around 70-
80°F (21-27°C). Cold water
can shock the roots and cause
damage.

5. Use filtered or distilled water: Orchids are sensitive to minerals and chemicals found in tap water, so it's best to use filtered or distilled water. If tap water is your only option, allow it to sit for 24 hours to allow the chlorine to evaporate.

6. Water thoroughly: When watering, be sure to thoroughly saturate the potting mix, allowing the water to drain out the bottom of the pot. This ensures that all the roots receive moisture and prevents salt buildup in the potting mix.

7. Avoid getting water on the leaves: Water droplets on the

leaves can magnify the sunlight and cause leaf burn. To avoid this, direct the water towards the potting mix and avoid getting water on the leaves.

8. Check for drainage: Orchid pots should have adequate drainage holes to allow excess water to escape. If the pot does not have enough drainage, the roots may become waterlogged and begin to rot.

9. Adjust watering during different seasons: Orchids may require more or less water depending on the season. During the summer, when temperatures are higher

and humidity is lower, orchids may require more frequent watering. During the winter, when temperatures are cooler and humidity is higher, orchids may require less frequent watering.

10.   Use a humidity tray: If you live in a dry climate, using a humidity tray can help increase the humidity around the orchid. Fill a tray with pebbles and water, and place the orchid pot on top.

11.   Watch for signs of overwatering: Overwatering is a common problem with orchids and can lead to root rot. Signs of overwatering include yellowing leaves,

mushy or brown roots, and a sour smell. If you suspect overwatering, reduce the frequency of watering and allow the potting mix to dry out more between waterings.

12. Watch for signs of underwatering: Underwatering can also be a problem with orchids and can lead to wilted or drooping leaves. If you suspect underwatering, increase the frequency of watering and ensure that the potting mix is thoroughly moistened.

13. Use the right watering technique. One effective method is to submerge the entire pot in a container of

room temperature water for 10-15 minutes, then allowing it to drain completely.

14.   Be mindful of the type of water you use. Orchids prefer water that is low in minerals and chemicals. Rainwater, distilled water, and reverse osmosis water are all good options.

15.   Don't let the orchid sit in water. After watering, be sure to dump out any excess water in the saucer or cachepot to prevent the roots from sitting in standing water.

16.   Consider the humidity in your environment. Orchids thrive in humid

environments, so if your home is particularly dry, you may need to water your orchid more frequently.

17. Pay attention to the temperature of the water. Orchids prefer water that is close to room temperature, so avoid using very cold or very hot water.

18. Water less in the winter. During the winter months when the orchid is in its dormant phase, you can reduce the frequency of watering to prevent overwatering.

19. Monitor the health of your orchid. If the leaves are drooping or the roots are

mushy, it may be a sign of overwatering. If the leaves are wrinkled or the potting mix is dry, it may be a sign of underwatering.

20.	Use a watering can with a long spout to water the orchid. This allows you to water the base of the plant without getting water on the leaves, which can cause rot.

CHAPTER 6

Avoiding Mistakes in Watering Orchid

Watering orchids is an important aspect of caring for them, and it's easy to make mistakes if you're not careful.

1. Overwatering: One of the most common watering mistakes is overwatering. This can lead to root rot and other fungal problems. To avoid overwatering, make sure the pot has good drainage and only water the orchid when the potting mix is dry to the touch.

2. Underwatering: Orchids can also suffer from underwatering, which can cause the leaves to become wrinkled and dry. To avoid underwatering, make sure to water the orchid regularly, especially during the growing season.

3. Inconsistent watering: Orchids can be sensitive to changes in watering patterns, so it's important to water them consistently. Try to water your orchid at the same time each week to avoid fluctuations in moisture levels.

4. Using the wrong type of water: Orchids prefer water

that is low in minerals and chemicals. Avoid using tap water, which can contain chlorine and other additives. Instead, use rainwater, distilled water, or reverse osmosis water.

5. Watering too frequently: Orchids do not need to be watered as often as other plants. Overwatering can lead to root rot and other fungal problems. To avoid this, only water your orchid when the potting mix is dry to the touch.

6. Watering too little: Orchids still need water, even if they don't need it as often as other plants. Make sure to water

your orchid regularly, especially during the growing season.

7. Watering at the wrong time of day: Watering your orchid in the evening can lead to fungal growth. Instead, water your orchid in the morning to allow any excess water to evaporate throughout the day.

8. Watering the leaves: Water on the leaves can cause fungal problems and other issues. When watering your orchid, make sure to water the potting mix and not the leaves.

9. Watering too fast: Pouring water too quickly can cause the potting mix to become

saturated, which can lead to root rot. To avoid this, pour water slowly and evenly over the potting mix.

10.   Watering too much at once: If the potting mix is very dry, it can be tempting to pour a lot of water on it all at once. However, this can lead to runoff and uneven moisture levels. Instead, water your orchid slowly and evenly to ensure the water is absorbed evenly.

11.   Using cold water: Orchids prefer water that is close to room temperature. Using cold water can shock the roots and cause damage.

Instead, use water that is at room temperature.

12. Using hot water: Similarly, using hot water can also damage the roots. Make sure to use water that is at room temperature or slightly cooler.

13. Using water that is too hard: Hard water can contain minerals that can build up in the potting mix and harm the orchid. Avoid using hard water and instead use rainwater, distilled water, or reverse osmosis water.

14. Watering during the dormant period: Orchids require less water during their dormant period, which is

typically in the winter. Make sure to adjust your watering schedule accordingly.

15.   Not adjusting watering for different seasons: Orchids have different watering needs during different seasons. During the growing season, they require more water than during the dormant period.

16.   Not adjusting watering for different types of orchids: Different types of orchids have different watering needs. Make sure to research the specific watering requirements of your orchid.

17.   Using a watering can that is too small: A small watering can can make it

18.   Overwatering: Overwatering is one of the most common mistakes made when caring for orchids. Orchids do not like to sit in standing water and their roots can easily rot if they are constantly wet. To avoid overwatering, make sure to let the potting mix dry out between waterings and only water when the top inch of the mix is dry to the touch.

19.   Watering at the wrong time: Watering orchids at the wrong time of day can also be detrimental. It is best to water in the morning so that any excess moisture can evaporate throughout the day. Watering at night can lead to

stagnant water and promote the growth of harmful bacteria.

20.   Not watering enough: While overwatering is a common mistake, not watering enough can also be a problem. Orchids need regular moisture to thrive, so make sure to water when the potting mix is dry. A good rule of thumb is to water once a week, but this can vary depending on the specific needs of your orchid.

21.   Not adjusting for environmental factors: The amount and frequency of watering needed for orchids can vary based on

environmental factors such as temperature, humidity, and air circulation. Make sure to adjust your watering schedule accordingly to ensure that your orchids are getting the right amount of moisture.

22.	Watering from the top: Watering from the top can lead to water pooling on the leaves and crown of the orchid, which can cause rot and disease. Instead, water from the bottom by placing the pot in a tray of water and letting the potting mix absorb the water.

23.	Inconsistent watering: Inconsistent watering can cause stress to the orchid and

lead to health problems.
Make sure to establish a
consistent watering schedule
and stick to it.

24.	Watering too
frequently during dormant
periods: During the dormant
period, orchids require less
water than during their active
growing season. Make sure to
adjust your watering schedule
accordingly to avoid
overwatering during this
time.

25.	Ignoring signs of
overwatering: Signs of
overwatering include
yellowing leaves, blackened
roots, and a mushy potting
mix. If you notice any of

these signs, adjust your watering schedule and allow the potting mix to dry out before watering again.

26.	Overfertilizing: Overfertilizing can lead to salt buildup in the potting mix, which can inhibit water absorption and cause dehydration. Make sure to follow the recommended fertilizing schedule for your orchids and flush the potting mix periodically to remove any excess salt buildup.

27.	Under fertilizing: While overfertilizing can be detrimental, under fertilizing can also lead to health problems for your orchids.

Make sure to provide your orchids with the necessary nutrients by fertilizing according to the recommended schedule.

28.   Using the wrong fertilizer: Orchids have specific nutrient requirements, so make sure to use a fertilizer that is designed for orchids. Using the wrong fertilizer can lead to nutrient deficiencies or excesses, which can cause health problems for your orchids.

29.   Fertilizing during the dormant period: Orchids require less fertilization during their dormant period.

Make sure to adjust your fertilization schedule accordingly to avoid overfertilizing during this time.

30.	Fertilizing when the potting mix is dry: Fertilizing when the potting mix is dry can cause root burn and other health problems. Make sure to water your orchids before fertilizing

CHAPTER 7

Diseases that can Affect Orchids and How to Fight Them

Orchids are a popular choice among gardeners and indoor plant enthusiasts because of their unique beauty and delicate appearance. However, orchids are also vulnerable to several diseases that can affect their health and appearance.

1. Bacterial Soft Rot: This bacterial disease can cause water-soaked, soft tissue that can turn brown or black. Overwatering or improper

drainage can cause this disease. To combat this disease, remove the infected parts of the plant and treat the remaining healthy parts with a copper fungicide.

2. Botrytis Blight: This fungal disease can cause brown or black spots on the leaves and flowers, along with a fuzzy gray mold. High humidity and poor air circulation can cause this disease. To fight this disease, remove the infected parts of the plant and treat the remaining healthy parts with a fungicide.

3. Fusarium Wilt: This fungal disease can cause yellowing and wilting of the leaves,

along with a brown discoloration of the stem. Poor soil drainage and overwatering can cause this disease. To combat this disease, remove the infected parts of the plant and treat the remaining healthy parts with a fungicide.

4. Leaf Spot: This fungal disease can cause small brown or black spots on the leaves, along with yellowing of the affected areas. High humidity and poor air circulation can cause this disease. To fight this disease, remove the infected parts of the plant and treat the remaining healthy parts with a fungicide.

5. Root Rot: This fungal disease can cause soft, brown or black roots that may have a foul odor. Overwatering or poor soil drainage can cause this disease. To combat this disease, remove the infected parts of the plant and repot the remaining healthy parts in fresh soil with proper drainage.

6. Viral Diseases: These are caused by viruses and can cause yellowing of the leaves and stunted growth. There is no cure for viral diseases, so the infected plant should be destroyed to prevent the spread of the virus to other plants.

7. Anthracnose: This fungal disease can cause brown or black spots on the leaves, along with a yellow halo. Overwatering or poor air circulation can cause this disease. To fight this disease, remove the infected parts of the plant and treat the remaining healthy parts with a fungicide.

8. Black Rot: This bacterial disease can cause black or brown spots on the leaves and flowers, along with a foul odor. Overwatering or poor air circulation can cause this disease. To combat this disease, remove the infected parts of the plant and treat the

remaining healthy parts with a copper fungicide.

9. Brown Spot: This fungal disease can cause brown spots on the leaves, along with yellowing and wilting. High humidity and poor air circulation can cause this disease. To fight this disease, remove the infected parts of the plant and treat the remaining healthy parts with a fungicide.

10. Cercospora Leaf Spot: This fungal disease can cause circular brown spots on the leaves, along with yellowing and wilting. High humidity and poor air circulation can cause this disease. To combat

this disease, remove the infected parts of the plant and treat the remaining healthy parts with a fungicide.

11.   Fusarium Crown Rot: This fungal disease can cause the collapse of the crown of the plant, along with a yellowing and wilting of the leaves. Poor soil drainage and overwatering can cause this disease. To fight this disease, remove the infected parts of the plant and treat the remaining healthy parts with a fungicide.

12.   Pythium Root Rot: This fungal disease can cause brown or black roots that may have a foul odor.

Overwatering or poor soil drainage can

13.	Rust: This fungal disease can cause orange or yellow spots on the leaves, along with yellowing and wilting. High humidity and poor air circulation can cause this disease. To fight this disease, remove the infected parts of the plant and treat the remaining healthy parts with a fungicide.

14.	Sooty Mold: This fungal disease can cause a black, sooty substance on the leaves and flowers. This is often a secondary infection resulting from honeydew produced by sucking insects such as aphids or mealybugs. To fight this disease, remove the insects with an insecticide and clean the plant with a mild soap solution.

15.	Southern Blight: This fungal disease can cause a white or yellowish growth on the stem of the plant, along with wilting and collapse. Poor soil drainage and overwatering can cause this disease. To combat this disease, remove the infected parts of the plant and treat the remaining healthy parts with a fungicide.

16.	Stem Rot: This fungal disease can cause a soft, brown or black stem that may

have a foul odor.
Overwatering or poor soil
drainage can cause this
disease. To fight this disease,
remove the infected parts of
the plant and treat the
remaining healthy parts with
a fungicide.

17.   Xanthomonas Leaf
Spot: This bacterial disease
can cause yellowing and
wilting of the leaves, along
with brown or black spots.
High humidity and poor air
circulation can cause this
disease. To combat this
disease, remove the infected
parts of the plant and treat the
remaining healthy parts with
a copper fungicide.

18.   Alternaria Leaf Spot: This fungal disease can cause brown spots on the leaves, along with yellowing and wilting. High humidity and poor air circulation can cause this disease. To fight this disease, remove the infected parts of the plant and treat the remaining healthy parts with a fungicide.

19.   Erwinia Soft Rot: This bacterial disease can cause water-soaked, soft tissue that can turn brown or black. Overwatering or improper drainage can cause this disease. To combat this disease, remove the infected parts of the plant and treat the

remaining healthy parts with a copper fungicide.

20.   Grey Mold: This fungal disease can cause gray or brown mold on the leaves and flowers, along with a softening and wilting of the affected areas. High humidity and poor air circulation can cause this disease. To fight this disease, remove the infected parts of the plant and treat the remaining healthy parts with a fungicide.

21.   Phytophthora Crown Rot: This fungal disease can cause the collapse of the crown of the plant, along with a yellowing and wilting of the leaves. Poor soil

drainage and overwatering can cause this disease. To combat this disease, remove the infected parts of the plant and treat the remaining healthy parts with a fungicide.

22.	Rhizoctonia Root Rot: This fungal disease can cause brown or black roots that may have a foul odor. Overwatering or poor soil drainage can cause this disease. To fight this disease, remove the infected parts of the plant and repot the remaining healthy parts in fresh soil with proper drainage.

23.   Sclerotinia Crown Rot: This fungal disease can cause the collapse of the crown of the plant, along with a yellowing and wilting of the leaves. Poor soil drainage and overwatering can cause this disease. To combat this disease, remove the infected parts of the plant and treat the remaining healthy parts with a fungicide.

24.   Tobacco Mosaic Virus: This viral disease can cause yellowing and stunting of the plant, along with distorted or mottled leaves. This virus can be transmitted by infected tools or hands. To prevent this disease, sterilize tools and wash hands before

handling orchids. There is no cure for this disease, so infected plants should be discarded.

25.	Orchid Necrosis Virus: This viral disease can cause necrosis or death of the tissue on the plant, along with stunting and distortion of the leaves. This virus can be transmitted by infected tools or hands. To prevent this disease, sterilize tools and wash hands before handling orchids. There is no cure for this disease, so infected plants should be discarded.

26.	Odontoglossum Ringspot Virus: This viral disease can cause ringspots on the leaves, along with stunting and distortion. This virus can be transmitted by infected tools or hands. To prevent this disease, sterilize tools and wash hands before handling orchids. There is no cure for this disease, so infected plants should be discarded.

27.	Cymbidium Mosaic Virus: This viral disease can cause mosaic patterns on the leaves, along with stunting and distortion. This virus can be transmitted by infected tools or hands. To prevent this disease, sterilize tools and wash hands before handling orchids. There is no cure for this disease, so infected plants should be discarded.

28.　　　Fusarium Wilt: This fungal disease can cause the yellowing and wilting of the leaves, along with a soft, brown stem. Overwatering or poor soil drainage can cause this disease. To fight this disease, remove the infected parts of the plant and repot the remaining healthy parts in fresh soil with proper drainage.

29.　　　Pythium Root Rot: This fungal disease can cause a soft, brown or black root that may have a foul odor. Overwatering or poor soil drainage can cause this disease. To combat this disease, remove the infected parts of the plant and repot the remaining healthy parts in fresh soil with proper drainage.

30.	Verticillium Wilt: This fungal disease can cause the yellowing and wilting of the leaves, along with a brown discoloration of the stem. Poor soil drainage and overwatering can cause this disease. To fight this disease, remove the infected parts of the plant and repot the remaining healthy parts in fresh soil with proper drainage.

There are various diseases that can affect orchids, and prevention is always better than treatment. Proper care, including good air circulation, proper watering and fertilizing, and maintaining cleanliness can go a long way in preventing diseases. When a disease does occur, it is important to identify the specific disease and take the appropriate steps to treat it. This may involve removing infected parts of the plant, repotting in fresh soil, and using fungicides or insecticides as needed. With proper care and attention, orchids can thrive and remain beautiful for years to come.

CHAPTER 8

Repotting an Orchid

Repotting an orchid with air roots can seem daunting, but it is an important part of orchid care to ensure the health and vitality of the plant. Air roots are an important part of an orchid's natural growth, as they absorb moisture and nutrients from the air. When repotting an orchid with air roots, it is important to take care not to damage these delicate roots.

1. Choose the right pot: When repotting an orchid with air roots, it is important to choose a pot that is the right size for the plant. Orchids

prefer to be in a snug pot, so choose a pot that is only slightly larger than the existing pot. Make sure the new pot has good drainage holes to allow excess water to drain away.

2. Prepare the potting mix: Orchids require a well-draining potting mix that allows air to circulate around the roots. Choose a mix specifically formulated for orchids, or make your own by combining bark, perlite, and charcoal.

3. Soak the potting mix: Before repotting, soak the potting mix in water for several

hours to allow it to absorb moisture.

4. Remove the orchid from its existing pot: Carefully remove the orchid from its existing pot, taking care not to damage the air roots. Gently loosen any roots that are tightly bound to the potting mix.

5. Trim any dead or damaged roots: As you remove the orchid from its existing pot, take the opportunity to trim any dead or damaged roots. Use a sterile pair of scissors or pruners to cut away any roots that are brown, soft, or mushy.

6. Prepare the new pot: Place a layer of fresh potting mix in the bottom of the new pot, making sure to cover the drainage holes. Arrange the orchid in the pot, positioning it so that the air roots are exposed and facing outwards.

7. Fill the pot with potting mix: Fill the pot with potting mix, making sure to leave the air roots exposed. Gently press the potting mix around the roots to hold the plant in place.

8. Water the orchid: Once the orchid is repotted, water it thoroughly to settle the potting mix around the roots. Allow the excess water to

drain away, and place the orchid in a well-lit location with good air circulation.

9. Monitor the orchid: After repotting, monitor the orchid closely for signs of stress. It may take a few weeks for the plant to adjust to its new pot, but with proper care, it should begin to grow and thrive.

10.   Timing: Repotting should be done when the orchid is in its active growth phase, which is typically in the spring or early summer. Avoid repotting during the dormant phase, which is usually in the fall or winter.

11.	Soaking the roots: Before repotting, it can be helpful to soak the orchid's roots in water for a few hours. This will help to hydrate the roots and make them more pliable, which can make them easier to work with during the repotting process.

12.	Don't bury air roots: It is important to avoid burying air roots when repotting an orchid. These roots need to be exposed to the air in order to function properly. When filling the pot with potting mix, make sure to leave the air roots exposed and facing outwards.

13.   Keep the potting mix loose: Orchids prefer a loose, well-draining potting mix. Make sure to avoid packing the mix too tightly around the roots, as this can impede air circulation and lead to root rot.

14.   Choose the right location: After repotting, it is important to choose a location for the orchid that provides the right amount of light and humidity. Orchids prefer bright, indirect light and high humidity. Avoid placing the orchid in direct sunlight, as this can damage the leaves and flowers.

15.   Watering: Watering is an important part of orchid care, and it is especially important after repotting. Water the orchid thoroughly, allowing the excess water to drain away. Avoid letting the orchid sit in standing water, as this can lead to root rot.

16.   Fertilizing: After repotting, it is important to avoid fertilizing the orchid for a few weeks. This will give the plant time to adjust to its new pot and reduce the risk of fertilizer burn.

17.   Monitoring: After repotting, it is important to monitor the orchid closely for signs of stress. Watch for

wilting, yellowing leaves, or other signs of distress. If you notice any problems, adjust your care routine accordingly.

CHAPTER 9

Fertilizing your Orchids

Fertilizing your orchids is an important part of their care, as it provides essential nutrients that they may not receive from their growing environment alone. However, it is important to approach fertilization with caution, as too much fertilizer can be harmful to your orchids.

There are various types of fertilizers available for orchids, including liquid, powder, and granular formulations. It is important to choose a fertilizer specifically formulated for orchids, as they have unique nutrient requirements. Some orchid fertilizers may also contain additional trace minerals and micronutrients that are beneficial to the plant.

The frequency and amount of fertilizer you apply to your orchids will depend on several factors, including the type of orchid, the stage of growth, the potting medium, and the growing conditions. As a general rule, it is recommended to fertilize your orchids every two weeks during the growing season (spring and summer) and every four to six weeks during the dormant season (fall and winter). However, it is important to follow the specific instructions on the fertilizer label, as different formulations may have different application rates and schedules.

When applying fertilizer to your orchids, it is important to dilute the fertilizer to the recommended strength. Applying too much fertilizer can burn the roots and leaves of the plant, leading to stunted growth or even death. It is also important to avoid getting fertilizer on the leaves or flowers of the plant, as this can cause damage.

One common method of fertilizing orchids is the "weakly weekly" method, which involves applying a diluted fertilizer solution every week. This allows for a consistent, controlled release of nutrients to the plant without the risk of over-fertilization.

In addition to fertilizing, it is important to maintain good cultural practices to ensure the health of your orchids. This includes providing adequate light, water, and air circulation, as well as regular repotting and pruning as needed.